Fears & Revelations

Alias Reve

BookLeaf
Publishing

India | USA | UK

Presentation by *BookLeaf Publishing*

Web: www.bookleafpub.com

E-mail: info@bookleafpub.com

ISBN: 9789357448024

First edition 2022

DEDICATION

to my dearest K

this small collection is dedicated all to you

without you   these words of mine   would not exist

ACKNOWLEDGEMENT

I would like to humbly thank and acknowledge my professors here at the University of Mississippi, both past and present, for guiding me tirelessly toward success; my parents, for encouraging my creativity and passion; my sister, for imbuing me with competitive spirit; my grandfather Pete, for showing me unconditional love, always; and my partner, for never giving up on, and always believing in me.
A special thanks to everyone who, knowingly or not, has helped to shape both my creative endeavors and my life as I know it. I would not, and could not be where I am without you today.

(swallowing stones)

no voice
the silence guts you like a butcher's blade
right down the middle,
but there's nothing left to spill.
no voice
just the distant elegy of screams.
a hollow ribcage
blood black as ink—
no voice
vines within your veins
the earth calls. you try to answer, but
no voice
for as long as you can remember
you have been dead.

(souhait de mort)

intimate fear
lying listless, unaware
if i weren't so afraid—
       never mind.
there is no "you" anymore.
it is only me
       my bed
       my sheets
       my soul.
l'appel du vide
(the void calls)
even as i lie here
       i yearn to find some high place and plunge
from it.
isn't the word for that tragedy?
somehow i climbed down the cliffs to the bottom
       unknowing
it is not the elevation that kills you
       it is the fall.

(forbidden fruit)

Tell me, did you eat what was
        forbidden? Is that what
                you think?

You think Truth is
        forbidden knowledge?

Why should it be, then, that the
        knowledge of what makes you
        unmakes you?
You cannot bite Truth
        into pieces
        you can
        understand.

Yet you seek
        reality from within
                reality

                like a passing thought
        inside
the mind

You cannot
        perceive all there is.

Tell me, did you
        consume what was

forbidden?
Did you
        feast on
        flesh and
        blood?

Do you know what is real?

                Or is it Truth, instead, that
        consumes
you?

(dream)

in the dream, there were
boy's arms
white arms reaching attached from my shoulders,
unnatural, pale

in the dream, there were
boy's palms
white palms streaking white lines across the table,
cluttered, frantic

i was breathing,
in the dream.

is there air in dreams? what lives there? what dies?

in my dreams, the high never sticks, my
brain cannot prick with adrenaline unconscious—
so the low never goes, but my body knows
in my dreams, still, that time will
pass into an inaccessible dimension, vivid
in mind alone; highs heighten lows.

in the dream, there were
realities
that consciousness relegates to nightmare, discarded,
slipped beneath

into neurons, atoms, energy
where nothing lives and, lifeless, nothing dies

(unreality)

hallucination of life:
the living produce light
humans themselves, striated
colors cats can contemplate;
bioluminescence, heat from
cellular fire, chemicals all
       ordered and agreed

waive the scientific say:
we are but fragments of reality
piecing together in our pieced way
try to be objective
perspective, subjective
there is neither
       order nor agreement

oxygen, hallucinogen
       "whole reality"
oxymoron
       there is no such thing
         as life

(buckets)

tear out emptiness
take off a little more skin

there, blank as a slate.
mama, why isn't my picture beautiful like the others?

more mistakes.
it must be pristine
buckets of white paint

    white paint
    white paint

i've never known color.
it's empty here

buckets of empty.
mama, where has all the paint gone?

i use blood
always my blood
and when the blood's gone

    white paint
    white paint

buckets of white paint
there, blank as a slate.

(the boy who cried wolf)

the boy cries wolf,
      wolf
      wolf
but the villagers find nothing.
stupid boy, careless boy,
      liar.

the boy sees shadows,
      creeping
      lurking
from the treeline eyes emerge.
shifting here, searching there,
      finding

the boy who cowers,
      screams
      pleads
for he knows no other name than
cruel monster, fell creature,
      wolf.

the lingering light blinks blushing down
over the green-gray pines, the animal
scent of sheared sheep and petrichor
carried on the howling squall, as the

tiny rain-droplets fall soundlessly to
earth, drowned in the brush of the trees.
standing, staring, as the water hits
and soaks his hair and cloak

the boy turns toward the bordering wood,
      waiting
      watchful
until it returns, the yellow glow of
shining eyes, dripping jaws,
      teeth—

the boy cries wolf,
      wolf
      wolf
but the villagers find nothing.
no blood, no body,
      no boy.

(sunless)

underwater eyes, cold like
a rush, a gust of winter wind
white ice above
blue below,

wading,
wading,
wading through
the dusky evening night, endless expanse

fading though
the twilight-tinged formless light
yet pierces through
in sharp rays; sourceless light

for there is no sun
there is no sun
no sun
there is no sun inside it

(tyler durden)

unconcerned with murder, crime, poverty.
but what are celebrity magazines and consumerism to
a nonbeliever?
you don't realize it, but sheep don't exist
psycho boy.
we're all wolves dressed like idiots.

unconcerned with murder, crime, poverty?
you pretend to be everything they pretend to hate.
that's why they all love you.
tyler, tyler, tyler—
wolf among wolves.

unconcerned with murder, crime, poverty?
they want to be who you think you are, naked, kisses
and lye, hitting rock bottom.
take off your wool, man among men
devour them before they see
you're really worth hating.

unconcerned with murder, crime, poverty.
who has seen beneath your skin?
who could? who wants to? they know what
you preach: dehumanized
freedom. they are animals for want of you.

"now this," you say, "is a chemical burn."
and it's almost the same thing as love.

(original sin)

be yourself, they said
as if it were an answer—
but i am so many creatures
and yet there are infinities of that which i am not
still
i long for him, her, them.
for you, so desperately.
i stepped into the shower
tears to cry, fears to cry
tearlessly
beneath this searing artificial rain i—
i mourned them.
everything i will never be
everything that will never be
mine.
the original sin must have been greed
not envy, not wanting god's position, just greed, just
wanting everything
oh, lucifer.
you had it within you to create,
but not to be
you had everything he did, archangel of god's
frail design
yet you wanted to
          be
              more
and it destroyed you

(satisfy)

spineless i suppose
the way i pull the trigger
hoping for death
from an unloaded gun

if i were braver—
if i were better—
but i am prayerlessly afraid.

the sage says

"i must remind you of the world."
now gorge yourself upon its unrequited beauty,
and its unholy destruction in equal shares—
"its lives and deaths are not to burden you."

now quiet, now listen, lover that you are
i am your master.
i will tell you when you may die.

(dissolve)

passing from memory
       is the darkness and the terror
       the tremors, the weakness
your every sense is screaming—
       you are a coward.

passing from memory
       is the darkness and the terror.
       along with our monsters
we retreat into the abyss—
       and are no more.

(you)

there's been a death.
some intangible being inside me has died
i never saw him but
  i loved him
and now everything fades away except
  you.
you, the undefinable, the silhouette of a nightmare i
forgot
  nightmarishly beautiful, i am corrupt

there's been a death.
until the blood runs down my chest i never notice
i never saw the blade but
  i loved it
and now everything fades away except
  you.
you, the definite, the carved severity of
michaelangelo's marble

this is what has died
you make me see stars, my love
this trepidation has died
i no longer fear my claws, my love
this frightened child has died
and now everything fades away except
  you.

(personified)

Microcosm of the universe
Cosmic specter I adore—
Can we adjourn? Although
I never cease to hum your baleful melody.
Bring yourself to me you wild weary thing
You make me pray for death in the same breath as
fearing what it means to be alive, so I
split and spilt the heavy fabric of your soul.
Unraveled strands still splay across the floor.
I thought to kill you, pull your threads and choke out
your coherent agony, the will, the want that will not
be contained;
the Thanatos of you that dares to live.

Speak to me, muse, lover, brother, personhood itself
you are, and yet I cannot grasp you,
name you:
Bitch, you unimaginable terror, you unholy endeavor.
You are beauty and psychosis playing
vain and vile games and
I am woven back into your mending wounds
determined still to prove my sin-subtle emergence
That I am greater than the sum of your parts
that I am not fading
      That I am not and
         that I am.

(violates you)

take suggestions as commands
succumb to an equal being's plan
    raise no protest

overwhelm of skull and tongue and teeth
no images within to fashion into speech
    less or more concrete

spill intrusions into your void, a place
where you allow yourself one solid space
    one secret to possess

transform mentality into the more defined
provided chains it is easier to bind
    hands than mind

you must not forget that

life and warmth, passion, beauty, birth, love
exist outside of the inside of you
    raise one protest

you must not forget that

escape without action is futility, my love, your
cold cruel barricades built of terror serve
    only to trap you

you must not forget that

my love
fear is what
        violates you

(to live)

plunging through the atmosphere at
terminal velocity
piercing clouds and shattering sky
the setting sun subsumes you in its rose-hued glow

       ages transpired before you existed, and even
more will pass
       when you are gone.

mere moments remain, now.
air rushes against your freeflying form.
parting the bittersweet sea at this speed will be like
hitting concrete.

       where did you come from, pale being?
       has some cruel creature flung you from these
silver heights?

if gravity alone compels you
there's nothing left but to en
              joy
                the fall.

(existence)

for as long as you can remember
you have been alive

bound inside this body:
strong, fragile, composed
of light and energy,
bioluminescence
of the soul, you are
capable of wondrous movement
surrounded, entranced; abundant
life fills you, spills from you—
feel the beat of your heart—is it so cold?
can you bear witness to the wordless,
the already infinite, the vast expanse,
any emotion you possess, any thought—
why do you chase life? what has it done
to you? living is not in the act—
living is all; all is life; there is no death
except for birth, no *thing* that does not
already exist; for you are all of it at once—

for as long as you can remember
      you have been—
              Alive.

(sunlight)

and you were born from darkness—

for it is in darkness, in the cold dirt,
in the rich brown earth where you
first find roots, reaching down
into darkness, into the warmth of
the core, into the eternal embrace
holding you steady, safe, solid.

but in the spring comes rain, and
you do not know rain; you know rain
solely from the snow and streams who
melt, filter from mineral mountains,
meeting you down beneath the ground;
it could break you, split you, drown you.

instead instinct lets you slither from
your brittle body, away from roots,
away from earth, away from safe, and
into sight: green leaves, grass, blue of sky;
into sound: thunder, birdsong, breaths of wind;
into sense: a new birth, new warmth, new life—

and you are reborn into sunlight

(heaven, hell)

do you know how long eternity is?
i will paint the sunset skies in your blood
grind your bones into the pavement
grant the ocean mist the color of your eyes
i will come up gasping:
what do i believe in, if there is belief in this world to
be held,
if there is nothing but belief as the melody of your
life sings out—
or is it, in itself, a kind of faith
to manage the cold teeth of fear and the
warm sweet delicacy of passion mingled
together in open palms
to breathe and try to love and feel alive

(purpose)

the golden hour, gained through
gloomy afternoon
when light breaks through
swathes of ancient gray
the fingers of the goddess
stretching down
to meet the meeting of
the earth and sea
after the trembling bout
of autumn rain
has soaked the sandy shore
with cleansing cold

what is it, love, my heart,
why are there tears?
the sun and rain are
beings as you are;
they touch and feel
and rage and love for you;
they give themselves freely,
not as sacrifices but as gifts
to you, for you, and for themselves;
and if you wonder why
this love is given, imagine—
if you are not also made

to be looked upon and opened up and
      loved
then what is all the universe for

(onward and upward)

24

noisy cars
a city road
faces passing
eyes alight

silent souls
while we erode
days are passing
into night